MW00760406

HOW TO BE
CIVIL
IN AN
Uncivil
WORLD

CYNTHIA BASINET

ARCHWAY
PUBLISHING

Archway Publishing books may be ordered through booksellers or by contacting:

Archway Publishing
1663 Liberty Drive
Bloomington, IN 47403
www.archwaypublishing.com
1 (888) 242-5904

ISBN: 978-1-4808-9271-2 (sc)
ISBN: 978-1-4808-9272-9 (e)

Library of Congress Control Number: 2020912717

Print information available on the last page.

Archway Publishing rev. date: 7/21/2020

Oh, simple word, and tender word,
Do fill my soul as I approach
Yon fellow heart, whose mind is spurred
In other ways. Let no reproach

Be from my lips; for equity
Is how we're born in this fair land.
Please, let there be the best of me
E'en as I take Conviction's stand.

Perhaps their thoughts would then admit
That there is something good at rest:
An ever Want of Peace to be
Residing in our caring breast

If bitterness, or hatred's gall
Be quick allowed to plant their seeds,
Then all is lost in Failure's pall,
Preventing Progress, Vict'ry's deeds.

Oh, simple word, and tender word,
Do fill my soul in all I do.
Let Union be my great reward.
Let Understanding be my hew.

Paul L. White
Author of Heroeswest.com

Many decades ago, friend and Island record executive, Charlie Minor leaned over from his table at Mr Chow's in Beverly Hills and said I should write a book. "The World According to Cynthia" he decried. It was not meant as a snark and when political dialogue became divisive, this book seemed even more in need.

After a year of collecting and another year of more collecting the time seemed even more right when the stimulus check came from the American taxpayers to publish.

There is nothing political about empowerment and the civility that it creates.

I have only one goal in the publishing of these quotes, To see the World,

Rich in mind
RIch in heart.
Rich in resourcefulness.
Rich in grace.

Am grateful to Charlie for planting this seed, may God rest his soul.

—Cynthia

A voice heard is a
solution possible.

So with that in mind,

"UBR"

Up, Back & Relaxed.

"BBR"

Take a beat, breath
and remind yourself
of what you want.

You don't move on.
you move through.

See the world like an eagle.
Live it like an ant.

To peace with our
only true power.

When you think you've
hit rock bottom,

There are still seven
more floors.

*Displaced societies
are of value.*

Their issues are our issues.

It's never about the actual event but rather what it forces one to process.

I'd like to live in a world where artists are priceless and Wall Street is redundant.

Why now?

It takes all facets to make this world a diamond.

Kindness seems to
come from those who
have the least.

You mean there's
a front door?

I don't need to be treated
better than anyone else,
just stop treating me
less than anyone else.

You never age if you
keep love in your heart,
passion in your soul and
a twinkle in your toes.

You're exactly where you should be, so just breathe!

Just 'cause I don't
say nothing don't
make me a sap.

There ain't nothing wrong with wealth — it's just who paid for it that matters.

Wait. Did I just say
that out loud?
Okay GOOD!

A vision seen transports dimension.

Fighting for the right thing
is never the wrong thing.

That was so not needed
in my repertoire of
feelings today.

The only thing you
have to answer is the
honesty of love.

Of course you can get to
the top faster by stepping
on everyone, but doesn't
it make it kind of lonely?

Life and the journey is a multitude of baby steps that lose nothing when we help another walk.

My path would have no
stones if Others had
not shared theirs.

They could've lifted a finger.
Instead, they stuck it in.

*Old stories that do not
end only go deeper.*

"Turn the other cheek"
does not mean you
forget who slapped it.

I'd rather wear the face of poverty than a face of deceit.

A smile is the outward radiance of the heart.

If you think I'm an idiot,
wouldn't I be if I tried
to change your mind?

It's never about the actual event, but what it forces one to process.

If we keep judging women like books, no one would bother to read.

When you walk with love,
love doesn't walk on you.

Our enemies are who
we alienate and do not
embrace for they too are
part of the solution.

Smart enough to see it.
Strong enough to say it.

That was so not needed
in my repertoire of
feelings today.

The sun will always rise when you swing the bat again.

If you're waiting for someone to help you, you will never succeed.

The #1 rule is baseball: you
get to hit the ball back!

Believing the tale is so much
easier than living the real.

So used to nothing that
nothing don't mean nothing.

My journey is bigger
than I know.
I merely put on the shoes.

When the mind plays,
the heart soars.

A woman is more than the sum of her parts. She is the soul that holds her parts.

Keep out your fancy shoes.

Life is a battle fought
with a steel tongue
and an open heart.

Life is long.
Keep your overhead low
and your expectations high.

Force isn't yours. It's for all those forces forcing you to have force.

Make the most of the
road not offered to you.

If you want to know your enemy, bow your head.

All heals when one
is remembered.

Success is walking the tightrope of life and not looking down.

Power is diffusing anger
and fusing peace.

Life is a balance that occurs when all can participate and profit.

Life is the journey lived.

Stay strong with
an open heart.

Attractiveness is love
shining outwards.

Don't ever deny yourself the gift of what is in the hopes of collecting on what might.

They don't see who is
at fault. Only the fault.

Be ambitious.
Not competitious.

May love beam when you
most need steam.

You have to be seen
to be heard.

You may not get what you want, but you usually get the best of what you need.

If they ain't bringing you up,
they're bringing you down.

Real life is worth slowing down for.

There's always one person
who knows the truth.

There are no small moments. All interactions are an opportunity to shine.

Don't let the World change your reality.
Let your reality change the World.

Keep being the change
to change the change.

Go gentle.
worship your temple.

I'm not one of a million.
I'm one in a million.

Grassroots grow the strongest trees.

You will never know the
beauty of the future if you
choose to go backwards.

Stop thinking of what your life should be and start thinking of what your life could be.

Life is the dress rehearsal for heaven.

Only through pain
does empathy gain.

Give yourself the gift of love. It cost nothing and no one can take away.

Do right even when
others do you wrong.

Say nothing. Does nothing.

When you sell your soul
for nothing; it costs
you everything.

May the grace of God
continue to reside within you.

Life is the consequence of
circumstance and truth.

You didn't see me because
you didn't look up.

Get healthy.
Does healthy.

Want something different?
Do something different.

When all shout, whisper
to be heard.

Why didn't you say
something when it mattered?

When life seems like a
horse race, step back
from the gate.

Life isn't about what you had but rather what's to be had.

When you know your heart,
you know your part.

*It's not a race so set
your own pace.*

Life isn't always good times and bad times don't last for good.

When you want to stand out
from the crowd, you have
to stand up to the crowd.

See over a problem not be anchored by a problem.

Learn to live with less.
Learn to respect more.

Only God knows why
and the best we can
do is comply.

A quiet mind is the greatest
gift to one's soul.

Your head is the last place to keep a list. It just takes up space.

Say "Yes" to the
improv of life.

You just can't explain crazy.

Just smile and move on.

"Forever hearing rancor,
Forever hearing screams...
How my soul seeks anchor
In peacefully flowing streams.

Herein are words to soothe a
soul tortured by animosity, and
seeking harmonious relationships
in their endeavors."

Paul L. White
(Author of Heroeswest.com)

Author Cynthia Basinet

A renowned social change activist, Cynthia is a Nobel Peace Prize nominee who has used her musical and pop culture notoriety as a platform to draw attention to important issues like self-determination, intellectual and copyright infringement and human rights, with an emphasis on the environment, refugees, women, children, the arts, mental health and disabilities, addiction and recovery.

This is her first book.

"Basinet is truly one of the great voices of our time."
-Matt Wong (PleasePassTheIndie.com)